AF869154

Baritone T.C.

FIRST DIVISION BAND COURSE

CONCERT FUN

by JAMES D. PLOYHAR, FRANK ERICKSON, ERIC OSTERLING, JOHN EDMONDSON, GERALD SEBESKY and JIM DUFF

CONTENTS

Published for

Conductor	FDL02022	3rd B♭ Trumpet	FDL02036
Flute	FDL02023	1st Horn in F	FDL02037
1st B♭ Clarinet	FDL02024	2nd Horn in F	FDL02038
2nd B♭ Clarinet	FDL02025	3rd Horn in F	FDL02039
3rd B♭ Clarinet	FDL02026	1st Trombone	FDL02040
B♭ Bass Clarinet	FDL02027	2nd Trombone	FDL02041
Oboe	FDL02028	3rd Trombone	FDL02042
Bassoon	FDL02029	Baritone T.C.	FDL02043
1st E♭ Alto Saxophone	FDL02030	Baritone B.C.	FDL02044
2nd E♭ Alto Saxophone	FDL02031	Tuba	FDL02045
B♭ Tenor Saxophone	FDL02032	Drums	FDL02046
E♭ Baritone Saxophone	FDL02033	Timpani	FDL02047
1st B♭ Trumpet	FDL02034	Bells	FDL02048
2nd B♭ Trumpet	FDL02035		

FOREWORD

In CONCERT FUN we present a group of concert band numbers, written and arranged by the country's leading band writers in the young band field. All numbers have been carefully selected for musical quality, student and audience appeal, and arranged with careful consideration of the playing abilities of the young bandsman. This collection is correlated to the FIRST DIVISION BAND METHOD PART TWO or any other second level band method.

FESTIVE SPIRIT

BARITONE T.C.

ERIC OSTERLING

BARITONE T.C.

SHOUT AMEN!

GERALD SEBESKY

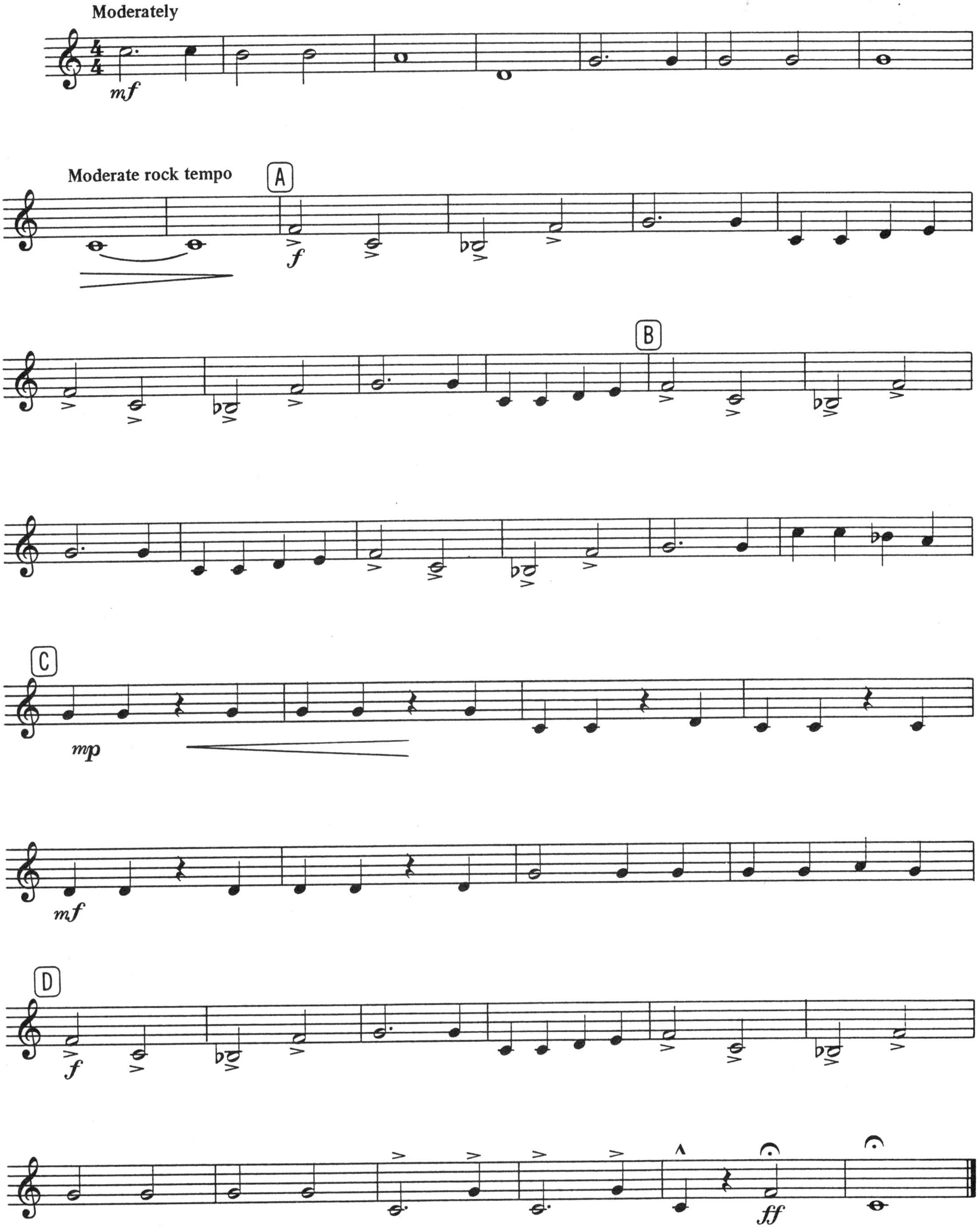

BARITONE T.C.

CHOP STICKS

Arranged by JAMES D. PLOYHAR

BARITONE T.C.

WALKIN' HOME

By GERARD BLACKMORE
Arranged by JIM DUFF

SEE, THE CONQUERING HERO COMES

BARITONE T.C.

G.F. HANDEL
Arranged by FRANK ERICKSON

BARITONE T.C.

MAMBO FROM THE CONGO

GERALD SEBESKY

BARITONE T.C.

THE MARINE'S HYMN

Official Song of the
United States Marines
Arranged by JAMES D. PLOYHAR

BARITONE T.C.

MISTY BLUE

ERIC OSTERLING

BARITONE T.C.

TRUMPICO

JAMES D. PLOYHAR

BARITONE T.C.

BLUES BLUEPRINT

By JOHN EDMONDSON

BARITONE T.C. LITTLE BROWN JUG SWINGS

Arranged by JAMES D. PLOYHAR

BARITONE T.C.

ALPHA OVERTURE

By JOHN EDMONDSON

BARITONE T.C.

SANTA ESPANOL

Latin-Rock

Arranged by JAMES D. PLOYHAR

BARITONE T.C.

A PURCELL SUITE

Arranged by FRANK ERICKSON

I. March

Allegretto

II. Irish Tune

Andante

III. Trumpet Tune

Allegro non troppo